GIRLS' HEALTH ™

SKIN CARE

SABINA K. JAWORSKI AND ROBERT CHEHOSKI

rosen publishing's
rosen
central®

NEW YORK

Published in 2012 by The Rosen Publishing Group, Inc.
29 East 21st Street, New York, NY 10010

Library of Congress Cataloging-in-Publication Data

Jaworski, Sabina K.
Skin care / Sabina K. Jaworski, Robert Chehoski. — 1st ed.
     p. cm. — (Girls' health)
Includes bibliographical references and index.
ISBN 978-1-4488-4574-3 (library binding)
1. Skin—Care and hygiene—Juvenile literature. I. Chehoski, Robert. II. Title.
RL87.J39 2012
646.7'2—dc22

                                                        2011006338

Manufactured in the United States of America

CPSIA Compliance Information: Batch #S11YA: For further information, contact Rosen Publishing, New York, New York, at 1-800-237-9932.

CONTENTS

INTRODUCTION

As young children, most girls don't give a tremendous amount of thought to their skin. When you were little, parents or guardians helped you stay clean and helped care for your skin. On occasion, you may have had a cut, scrape, or rash, which was unpleasant for the moment, but then went away quickly.

As you approach and enter the teen years, caring for the skin can suddenly seem a lot more complicated. If you like to read teen magazines, you will likely be bombarded with advertisements for skin care products to make you look more beautiful. You and your friends may become self-conscious about hair growth, discovering that skin is something people expect you to shave and pluck. Acne may start to appear on your skin (about three-quarters of teens experience it!), giving you something new to worry about and manage.

This book explores what you need to know about caring for your skin during this challenging time. The first chapter explains the science of how skin works as an organ. The text then provides helpful advice about everyday skin care, including choosing products, maintaining a skin-friendly diet, and protecting against sun damage. You'll also learn how to deal with acne and other skin conditions.

If you find skin care frustrating, remember: skin is a living organ, and it's okay if your skin isn't always perfect. Even the actresses and models you see in magazines and films do not always have perfect skin. They usually spend a long session having makeup professionally applied before their shoots. Then, if there are still visible imperfections, the photographers can airbrush or alter the images to make the skin look perfectly even. This is an impossible standard to reach in real life.

Skin care is important, but strong self-esteem and positive relation-
ships will help you glow from within.

CHAPTER one

UNDERSTANDING SKIN

The skin is the body's largest organ, and it serves a variety of purposes. Not only does skin cover the largest area of any organ, but it is also the heaviest organ, accounting for 15 percent of our body weight. Skin is part of the integumentary system, which keeps the body intact. Skin helps protect us from our environment, helps regulate our body temperature, and helps us get rid of bodily waste products. Skin also provides us with the ability to experience different types of sensations, including touch, temperature, and pain.

STRUCTURE OF THE SKIN

Skin is made up of three main layers: the epidermis (the top layer), the dermis (the middle layer), and the subcutaneous tissue. The epidermis helps guard against infection and provides the body with a waterproof shield. It is comprised of two types of cells: basal cells and squamous cells. The epidermis is divided into five sublayers, or strata.

Below the epidermis is the dermis, which is made up of two layers of connective tissue: papillary tissue and reticular tissue. The dermis is full of blood and lymphatic vessels, nerve fibers, sweat glands, sebaceous or oil glands, and hair follicles.

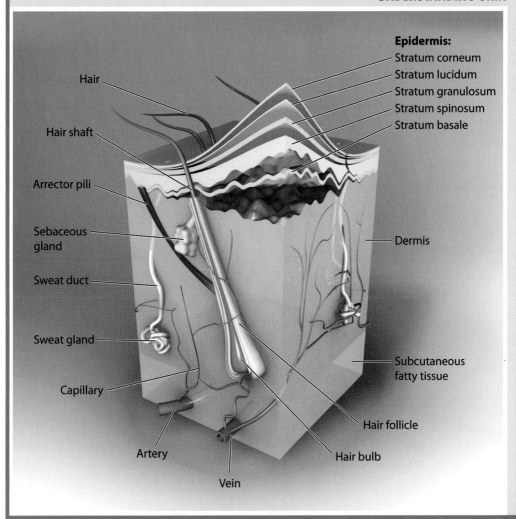

Hair

Hair shaft

Arrector pili

Sebaceous gland

Sweat duct

Sweat gland

Capillary

Artery

Vein

Epidermis:
Stratum corneum
Stratum lucidum
Stratum granulosum
Stratum spinosum
Stratum basale

Dermis

Subcutaneous fatty tissue

Hair follicle

Hair bulb

This cross section of the skin shows the three main skin layers and the structures within them. The epidermis, dermis, and subcutaneous tissue appear in peach, pink, and green.

Below the dermis is a layer of subcutaneous (beneath the skin) tissue. The subcutaneous layer contains fat cells called adipocytes. This fat provides insulation for the body. Fifty percent of the fat in the body is found in this subcutaneous layer of skin. This layer also contains blood vessels, nerves, the roots of oil and sweat glands, and hair roots.

Each layer of skin is made up of skin cells. Your body replaces skin cells each day in a process of continuous shedding. Basal cells are long and thin and are found in the bottom layer of the epidermis. As basal cells reproduce, there is not enough room for the new cells, so some of the cells are pushed toward the top of the epidermis. As they move upward, the basal cells flatten and turn into squamous cells. When squamous cells reach the top of the epidermis, they form a thick layer called the cornified layer, or stratum corneum. When the process is complete, skin cells are shed. In this way, new skin cells constantly replace old ones.

A PROTECTIVE BARRIER

Skin provides a barrier between the internal tissues and organs in the body and the external environment. Skin protects us not only from visible particles such as dirt, but also from microscopic disease-causing organisms such as bacteria. Among the cells in your skin are immune cells that capture and destroy microorganisms that might be harmful to the body. Many common types of bacteria are constantly being deposited on your skin from the earth, water, and solid objects with which you come in contact.

If you are healthy and maintain normal cleanliness by washing daily, then your immune system should be perfectly capable of protecting you from common bacteria. Normal soap will eliminate most bacteria you encounter. Frequent hand washing with soap and water can protect you from the transmission of germs that can cause sickness. However, for most healthy people, the use of antibacterial soaps and other products may do more harm than good. This is so because there are always some bacteria that are resistant to (not affected by) the antibacterial compound. These bacteria survive and reproduce—and they do so quickly. As each generation of resistant bacteria multiplies, there will soon be hundreds, then thousands, then millions of resistant bacteria. Then, when people get sick

A basic hygiene routine includes frequent hand washing, showering or bathing daily in warm water, and washing the face in the morning and evening with a mild cleanser.

or injured and bacteria gets into their systems, the antibiotics that we rely on to kill bacteria won't work. For this reason, antibacterial products should be used only when absolutely necessary, and ordinary soap and water should be used daily.

A TEMPERATURE REGULATOR

Skin helps regulate body temperature in two ways. First, the skin contains sweat glands. Water is excreted (expelled) from the sweat glands onto the

When the body becomes overheated, such as during vigorous activity, sweat glands in the skin give off perspiration. As the moisture evaporates, the body cools off.

surface of the skin, where it evaporates and cools the body. The skin also contains many blood vessels. These vessels allow more blood to flow through the skin than is needed to provide nourishment and remove waste products. The body uses these blood vessels to control heat loss and maintain a proper temperature. When the body is hot, the blood vessels dilate, or expand, allowing more blood to reach the surface of the skin, where heat is lost through radiation. When we are exposed to cold, the blood vessels contract, allowing less blood to reach the surface. This helps the body retain heat.

A SOURCE OF INFORMATION

Skin contains specialized cells that transmit different types of sensory information. There are sensory cells for pain, temperature, pressure, and vibration. Each type transmits information along nerves to the brain, providing information about the environment around the body. There are more than one thousand nerve endings in 1 square inch (6.45 square centimeters) of skin.

In addition to transmitting information to us, skin can provide information about us to others. When people experience strong emotions, the body responds. For example, when we experience shock, blood vessels contract, reducing the amount of blood near the surface of the skin, causing us to look pale. In contrast, when we are embarrassed, we blush because the anxiety we experience causes the body to respond as if we are threatened. The blood vessels expand to provide more blood to the muscles in case we need to fight or flee.

A small amount of sun exposure helps the body make vitamin D. For more than five to fifteen minutes in the sun, wear protective clothing and sunscreen to prevent skin damage.

SKIN'S METABOLIC ROLE

Skin helps regulate our internal body functions, a process also known as metabolism. When ultraviolet (UV) light from the sun reacts with elements in the skin, the body is able to synthesize, or make, important vitamins such as vitamin D. Vitamins are critical for the body to function normally. For example, a lack of vitamin D can lead to osteopenia, which is a milder version of osteoporosis, a thinning and weakening of the bones. Lack of vitamin D can also cause muscle weakness. The skin stores lipids (fats) and water, which helps us maintain the right amount of moisture in the body for good health. Skin is not totally waterproof, however, and small amounts of toxins and bodily waste products, such as urea, pass through the skin and evaporate.

CHAPTER two

EVERYDAY SKIN CARE

Most girls know how to properly care for their skin by washing daily with soap and water and following with a body moisturizer. Unless you have a special condition of the skin, such as psoriasis, eczema, or rosacea, this section will help you understand how to meet your general skin-care needs.

HEALTHY SKIN IS BEAUTIFUL SKIN

Maintaining a proper diet is the best way to maintain healthy skin. If you eat a variety of healthy foods—vegetables and fruits; breads and cereals; milk, yogurt, and cheese; meat, poultry, fish, legumes, eggs, and nuts—your body will get the many nutrients that it needs. Also, drink lots of water. Water helps to flush out impurities, or things that can harm your skin. It also keeps your skin hydrated and healthy.

Getting adequate exercise is also beneficial to your skin. Aerobic exercises such as running, swimming, and cycling are some of the best ways for you to stay in shape. The word "aerobic" literally means "with oxygen." Aerobic exercise increases blood flow throughout the body. This helps to ensure that the tissues get the oxygen they need and the cells have their wastes efficiently removed. When you sweat, impurities are brought up through the skin where they can be removed.

Having a well-balanced diet with plenty of colorful vegetables and fruits is one of the keys to maintaining healthy skin.

CHOOSING PRODUCTS

To keep your skin healthy and glowing, it's important to keep it clean. Be sure to check the ingredients in any soap, facial astringent, moisturizer, or mask that you use. Watch out for ingredients that might cause an allergic reaction. If you develop a rash or blemishes after trying a particular product, stop using it at once. It may be helpful to go to a dermatologist (a doctor specializing in skin care) if a problem persists.

These days, nearly every company that makes cosmetics also has a line of skin-care products. Do you really need a company's entire line, including facial wash, toner, night cream, day cream, serum, and exfoliant? In most cases, your skin-care regime can be limited to cleanser, water, and a good moisturizer. Teens who have trouble with oily skin can use toner, which helps eliminate oil and control acne breakouts. Witch hazel is an inexpensive substitute.

When you're an adult, you might find some of the other products useful, but for now, plain facial cleansers should be enough to keep your skin looking good. If you have acne—and most teens have at least a little—don't look for miracle cures at the makeup counter. Instead, try a drugstore product with acne fighters like benzoyl peroxide or salicylic acid. You can also ask your dermatologist to recommend a product that will help.

PROTECTING YOUR SKIN

Exposure to the sun causes skin to dry out, become coarser, and wrinkle over time. UV radiation from the sun is the most common cause of skin cancer. Whenever you are exposed to sunlight for a significant period, you should use a sun-blocking lotion or cream. Sunscreens have a number called the sun protection factor (SPF) on the label that signifies how effective the product is at blocking ultraviolet radiation. The higher the number, the more protection the product provides. You should always use a sunblock with an SPF of 15 or higher. If you tend to burn easily, look for an SPF of 30 or higher. Use sunblock even on cloudy days if you will be outdoors, as ultraviolet light can penetrate cloud coverage.

The harsh, cold winds of winter can dry out skin, as can the heating systems we use to keep our homes warm. If skin dries out too much, it can crack and peel. To help prevent skin from drying out, moisturizers can be used. These are lotions or creams that are applied to the surface of the skin to keep moisture inside. They typically contain oil- or water-based compounds to seal moisture into the skin. Despite the claims of some products, moisturizers do not put water back into your skin. However, they can be helpful in keeping it from escaping. Lip balm is a thick form of moisturizer that contains wax to help seal the surface of the lips.

To safely enjoy going to the beach or pool, apply sunscreen to protect your skin from dangerous UV rays. Reapply sunscreen every ninety minutes to two hours and after swimming.

A GUIDE TO SKIN TYPES

In addition to following the general advice above, you may need to make a skin-care plan based on your overall skin type. Below is a guide to the various skin types. You may find that you fit into one category almost all of the time, or you may find that the quality of your skin changes based on the time of the year.

- **Normal skin** is characterized by an even tone and smooth surface. Acne is not usually a problem.
- **Dry skin** typically does not retain moisture and has a parched look. The skin feels tight after washing with soap and water. Acne may be an issue, although blemishes are more common among those with oily skin.

- **Oily skin** is usually shiny because the sebaceous glands are overactive. If you have oily skin, you likely have the blemishes and blackheads that are associated with the production of extra sebum—oily matter that lubricates skin.
- **Combination skin** is typically characterized by dry skin on the cheeks and oily skin on the forehead, nose, and chin— otherwise known as the T-zone.

CARING FOR NORMAL SKIN

Most people have some skin on their body that they would describe as "normal": it's not too oily or too dry. Care for normal skin requires nothing

To help prevent acne, remove makeup before bed with a gentle cleanser or makeup remover. If you are prone to breakouts, use cosmetics that are labeled noncomedogenic.

more than daily washing, weekly exfoliating (using a special cleansing mitt or scrub to slough off dead skin cells), and applying an occasional moisturizer. Maintaining a healthy diet of fresh fruits and vegetables, lean meats or fish, and plenty of water will help keep your skin looking great. Also, getting adequate rest (at least eight hours per night) will keep your skin looking its most radiant. Exercise can also keep your skin glowing. Avoid smoking cigarettes, which can age and discolor the skin.

No matter what skin type you have, everyone should apply sunscreen to the face and body before heading out of doors. Exposure to UV rays can prematurely age the skin and increase a person's risk of skin cancer. Any time you discover an unusual marking on your skin that

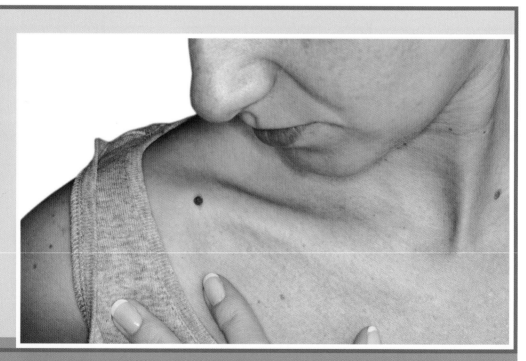

A mole that changes size, shape, color, or texture can be a sign of skin cancer. Become familiar with the appearance of your moles and birthmarks, and check to see if they change.

doesn't heal, or that changes in size or color, you should bring it to the attention of a doctor.

CARING FOR OILY SKIN

Oily skin, common in teens and young adults because of rapidly changing hormones, can be quite challenging to control. In most cases, oily skin is caused by overactive sebaceous glands. This is a trait that is inherited from your parents. The good news is that oily skin is often slower to wrinkle and show the signs of aging.

In order to keep your oily skin looking fresh, you must wash frequently with cleanser and water. If you tend to sweat a lot, dress in lightweight cotton clothing that allows the skin to excrete normally. Avoid wearing man-made fabrics that contain polyester, nylon, or acrylic, as these may cause the body to perspire. Instead, wear fabrics that are 100 percent cotton or made with a cotton blend. If oily skin on your face is a problem, consider wiping your face frequently with premoistened cleansing pads. There are many commercially manufactured disposable wipes available, or you can make your own. Fill a small plastic zipper bag with cotton balls and lightly sprinkle them with witch hazel or your favorite toner. You can also carry oil-blotting sheets to absorb extra oil during the day. Last, use only moisturizers and sunscreens that are oil-free and noncomedogenic (unlikely to clog pores).

CARING FOR DRY SKIN

People are most affected by dry skin during the winter and summer months, though some are affected by dry skin no matter the weather conditions. Your environment can contribute a great deal to dry skin. People are often affected by living in conditions that are bombarded with an excess of dry heat, which lacks humidity or moisture. If you are afflicted with chronic dry skin, then your parents probably had similar traits.

Trying products that smell or feel nice on the skin or that come in pretty packages can be fun. However, most girls need only a few basics, such as cleanser, moisturizer, and sunscreen.

There are ways to combat dry skin. Avoid washing your face with harsh cleansers and exfoliants. Drink plenty of fluids, and wash no more than twice a day. When you do shower, do so in warm—not hot—water. Hot water dries out the skin. Following a shower or bath, pat your skin with a towel and apply an oil-based moisturizer while your skin is still damp. This will help maintain a layer of moisture for a longer period. Special moisturizers for dry skin, such as those containing colloidal oatmeal, may help. Finally, if you can, add moisture to the air by adding a humidifier to your bedroom.

MYTHS
AND FACTS

MYTH **Acne is made worse by a girl's diet, especially if she eats fried foods or chocolate.**

FACT While a healthy diet can improve the skin's overall appearance, eating certain foods has nothing to do with a girl's chance of developing acne. The main cause of acne is an increase in sebum production. This is related to changes in hormone levels during puberty and is often genetic.

MYTH **You can shrink large pores if you use commercially prepared toners and masks.**

FACT Once the skin's pores are enlarged, they cannot "shrink," no matter which products you use. Washing your face often will help keep pores cleaner, and they will appear less enlarged, but pores do not contract, nor can they be extracted to decrease in size.

MYTH **If you are young, you don't need to take precautions against developing skin cancer.**

FACT People of all ages need to take precautions against skin cancer. Sun exposure during youth can contribute to skin cancer down the road. Melanoma, a common and deadly skin cancer, largely affects people in their twenties. Despite rising rates of skin cancer, only about 34 percent of young adults use sunscreen, according to the American Academy of Dermatology. The facts are obvious: all people need to apply sunscreen liberally to exposed skin whenever they are going to be outside. A good solution is to use a daily moisturizer with an SPF of at least 15.

CHAPTER three

DEALING WITH ACNE

Seventy-three percent of teens between age twelve and nineteen suffer from acne and acne-related breakouts. Acne also affects some adults. Acne is a skin disease that affects the follicles, or pores, that cover your face and body.

WHAT IS ACNE?

A follicle is a tiny duct in the skin where a hair grows. Inside each follicle, at the bottom of the hair, is a sebaceous gland. This gland produces oil called sebum. Sebum travels up the hair and onto the skin. It is needed to keep your skin and hair healthy.

Usually the sebaceous glands produce a normal amount of sebum. In people who suffer from acne, though, the glands produce an excess of oil. (Heredity plays a part in who will develop acne. If your parents suffered from frequent breakouts, chances are you will, too.) Too much sebum causes the follicles to become sticky and clogged with oil and dead skin. Bacteria on the skin mix with the oil and get into the follicles. The bacteria cause the follicles to become infected, and the follicles become red and inflamed. This inflammation causes swelling and redness. The inflamed pore is a skin blemish known as an acne lesion.

Acne can be an upsetting condition that can make a girl want to hide. A dermatologist can discuss options for treating acne and making it less noticeable.

Acne most often occurs on the face, back, neck, shoulders, upper arms, and chest. These areas of the skin have the highest concentration of oil glands and therefore produce more sebum than other parts of the body. Where there is more sebum, there is a greater chance of acne appearing.

On the face, the oil glands are more concentrated in an area called the T-zone, which runs across the forehead and down the nose to the chin. This T-shaped area is where you are most likely to break out. Here, the skin is oilier and the pores tend to be larger than on other parts of the face. However, acne can also show up on the cheeks, jawline, and neck.

THE ROLE OF HORMONES

Teens are prone to developing acne because hormones are working to activate physical changes in the body. Hormones are chemical substances that help people grow and develop. Yet these same hormones can also result in side effects such as voice changes, hair growth, and acne. Acne usually starts when a young person enters puberty, the stage in which you begin developing adult characteristics. For females, this is generally around age eleven. Males start puberty at about age thirteen.

A particular kind of hormone called an androgen is one of the main causes of acne. Androgens are male sex hormones produced by the body. Androgens are present in both males and females. They cause the sebaceous glands to become larger and produce more oil. This process is normal in all teenagers. However, if you suffer from acne, the androgens in your body are telling your sebaceous glands to make too much oil.

In young women, there are hormonal changes that occur around the time of the menstrual cycle. Before menstruation, the ovaries make a hormone called progesterone. Progesterone helps a woman's body prepare for pregnancy. It also makes oil glands more sensitive. Androgens take advantage of this sensitivity, telling the glands to produce more oil. This hormonal activity is the reason that breakouts often happen from two to seven days before your period begins.

Hormonal changes during the menstrual cycle can trigger acne, as well as cramps. Acne lesions typically form a few days before one's period begins and go away when it is completed.

ACNE LESIONS

You may notice that you have several different kinds of acne. Some types of acne may look worse than others. They can be so severe that they may lead to scarring. There are four varieties of acne lesions. From the mildest to the most severe, they are comedones, papules, pustules, and cysts.

Comedones are basically clogged pores. Comedones form when the sebum in a hair follicle reaches the skin's surface. The sebum then becomes solid, like a plug, and blocks the pore. Comedones include whiteheads and blackheads. Whiteheads form when a plug of sebum closes up the pore and forms a tiny bump with a white center. A blackhead is a clogged pore with a dark center. The black center is not dirt, despite what people think. The change in color occurs because the pore has opened. The sebum plug has been exposed to the air and oxidized, which has turned it dark.

Papules and pustules are what most people call pimples, the raised, red bumps where the skin is inflamed. A papule or pustule forms when a follicle is completely blocked and oil becomes trapped under the skin. The oil starts building around the hair because it has nowhere to go. The blocked pore then becomes irritated and opens, allowing bacteria and dead skin cells to get under the skin. The bacteria under the skin cause inflammation, or swelling, in and around the follicle. The infection under the skin builds and swells. This results in a small red bump called a papule. If the bump is filled with pus, a yellowish white substance—full of dead cells and bacteria—it is called a pustule. Pustules are more severe than papules. The pus is a sign of infection.

Cysts, also called nodules, are the most severe kind of acne. Cysts are large, painful, pus-filled lumps that occur deep under the skin. If the inflammation is very severe, the pus can burst under the surface of the skin. This can lead to greater infection and more cysts. This kind of acne, called cystic or inflammatory acne, can lead to permanent scarring. Cysts

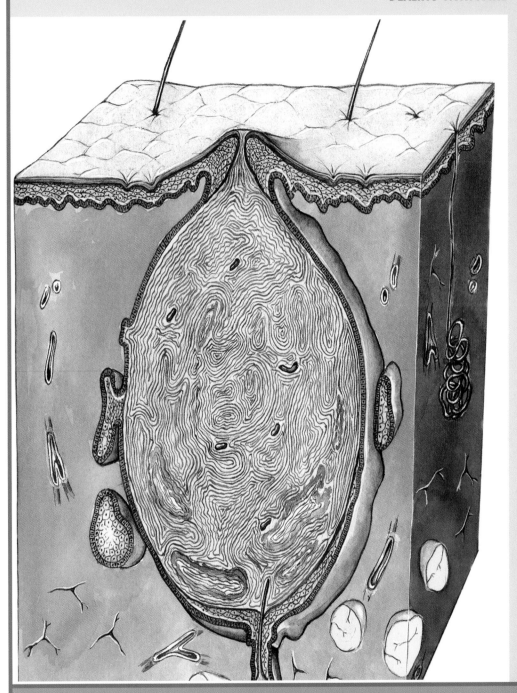

The basic acne lesion is the comedo, a blocked pore that becomes filled with sebum, skin debris, and bacteria. A closed comedo is commonly called a whitehead.

should never be squeezed. To help relieve the pressure or pain of a cyst, apply clean, warm compresses several times a day and take warm showers.

You may wonder why one pimple lasts for only a few days, while another can stay around for weeks. This happens because some acne lesions are more infected than others.

Generally, a papule lasts anywhere from five to ten days. Pustules usually last for five or six days, depending on how infected they are. Cysts can last for several weeks or even months. If a cyst does not heal within four weeks, bring it to the attention of your doctor.

PREVENTING ACNE

There is only one cause of acne: too much sebum is being produced by the oil glands in the skin. Unfortunately, it is not always possible to prevent this from occurring. However, there are several things you might be doing to make your acne worse. Being more careful about these things may cut down on your breakouts.

First, while it is important to keep acne-prone skin clean, it is possible to overdo it. Washing too often can dry out your skin. Harsh soaps, such as scrubs or astringents, can also cause drying. The dry skin then produces more oil to replace the oil it has lost. With the production of this additional oil, breakouts are more likely.

Skin that has broken out is very delicate. If you scrub with a washcloth or face sponge, or if you use facial scrubs, you can make skin that is irritated even worse. Harsh scrubbing can also open up blemishes that are already on your skin. This increases the risk of more bacteria entering the blemish. Bacteria can cause the pimple to become more infected. In caring for acne-prone skin, sometimes less is more.

When choosing makeup and other skin products like lotions and sunscreens, be sure to pick products that are labeled oil-free, noncomedogenic, or nonacnegenic. They are formulated not to clog pores. Some makeup contains antiacne medicine, which can help prevent acne. Also, bacteria can grow in face sponges, makeup brushes, and washcloths. When you use them, bacteria can be transferred to your face. Therefore, always use clean washcloths and sponges. Cosmetic brushes should be cleaned frequently with soap and water and left to air-dry. Fingertips also carry oil, dirt, and bacteria. Wash your hands before applying makeup and other products to your face with your fingers.

If you are prone to acne, you'll want to be careful with hair products as well. Products such as gels, mousses, and sprays can aggravate acne, so keep them away from your face as much as you can. Hats, scarves, and headbands should be cleaned often, as they gather dirt and oil. Here are additional tips you can follow to help prevent acne breakouts:

- Resist the urge to tan. In the long run, the sun can actually cause more breakouts.
- Hold the phone away from your chin when talking, and clean phone surfaces frequently with rubbing alcohol. Avoid resting your head on your hands in class, when studying, or when watching television.
- Take a shower after you've been sweating, and use an anti-acne body wash.
- Remove workout clothes and athletic uniforms immediately after wearing them. Then shower as soon as possible. Keep your athletic equipment, especially pads and chin straps, clean.
- Shampoo your hair at least twice a week. Keep your hair off your face and shoulders with ponytail holders or barrettes, especially when you sleep.
- If your after-school job involves working in a hot kitchen with grease, take a shower immediately following your shift.
- Change your pillowcases regularly. Bacteria can grow in the fabric overnight and cause breakouts.

Picking and squeezing pimples is tempting, but it will only worsen the acne and possibly cause scarring.

SKIN PICKING

Resist the temptation to pick, squeeze, or pop blemishes. Squeezing a pimple can make it worse. First, it pushes some of the oil and bacteria in the blemish deeper into the skin. This can lead to more infection and make the pimple last longer. It can also cause the pimple to develop into a more severe cyst.

Second, squeezing a blemish doesn't allow it to heal. Instead, it exposes the lesion further. Bacteria and oil can get into the open blemish and cause a bigger infection. Touching and squeezing can also infect the surrounding skin and lead to more pimples.

Finally, you risk creating permanent scars if you pick or squeeze your acne. This is especially true if you squeeze a pimple long enough to see blood. Also remember: never pop or incise (slit open) a blemish with a pin or needle, even if it is sterilized.

OVER-THE-COUNTER PRODUCTS

For some teenagers, over-the-counter (OTC), or nonprescription, products will work to treat acne. The goal of all acne medications is to clear up acne and prevent new acne from forming. All over-the-counter treatments are topical, or used only on the surface of the skin.

You will find a number of different acne products at your local drugstore. You will probably need to experiment to find the treatment that works best for you. You may also choose to use a combination of acne products. However, keep in mind that using too many products or too much of one product may cause excessive dryness.

The choice of which products to use depends on what kind of acne you have, where the acne is on the body, and how severe it is. Read the labels of products to find out which type of acne-fighting ingredients they contain. The following ingredients can be found in cleansers, astringents, makeup, creams, lotions, gels, and facial masks:

- **Antibacterials.** Many body washes and soaps for treating acne are known as antibacterials because hey help kill *P. acnes*, the bacterium responsible for acne breakouts. Using antibacterials can sometimes lead to skin dryness, redness, and irritation.
- **Benzoyl Peroxide.** One of the most common treatments for mild acne, benzoyl peroxide kills the bacteria found in the follicles and helps treat inflamed pimples. It is available as a lotion, cream, gel, or cleanser and comes in 2.5 percent, 5 percent, and 10 percent strengths. Begin by using a low strength once or twice a day. This will allow your skin to adjust to the medication. When you apply benzoyl peroxide, avoid direct contact with clothing or sheets until the medication has dried. The peroxide can leave permanent bleach stains on fabrics.
- **Salicylic Acid.** This ingredient helps to slough off dead skins cells and works to unclog pores and prevent lesions. Unlike benzoyl peroxide, salicylic acid works best against

Cleansers containing benzoyl peroxide or salicylic acid can be effective in treating acne. Some natural remedies can be helpful as well.

whiteheads and blackheads. Side effects can include dry skin, peeling, and irritation.

- **Alpha-Hydroxy Acids (AHAs).** Typically found in lotions and creams, AHAs also go by other names, such as beta-hydroxy acids, fruit acids or extracts, and tri-alpha-hydroxy acids. All of these come from the natural acids found in fruit, sugarcane, and milk. AHAs work to remove dead skin cells, which helps prevent pores from clogging. Side effects include possible skin irritation or an allergic reaction.

NATURAL REMEDIES

You don't always have to rely on drugstore medications to deal with mild cases of acne. There are many natural remedies that can do wonders for your skin. The following are some popular natural remedies that you can make at home with everyday ingredients or purchase in a store:

- Facial masks absorb oil, tighten pores, and moisturize dry skin. You can make an at-home mask with clay, egg yolks, honey and oatmeal, or milk of magnesia.

- Tea tree oil from the melaleuca tree in Australia helps to kill acne-causing bacteria. It can be found in cleansers and astringents.
- Ice can be used to reduce redness and swelling. Wrap an ice cube in plastic wrap and hold it against the pimple for a few minutes. Repeat three times a day.
- Sulfur is a natural antiseptic. You can buy sulfur soaps that help to fight acne-causing bacteria.
- Steam your face by holding it over hot water. This helps to open up and unclog the pores. (Be careful that the water isn't too hot, though, since this can cause a steam burn.)
- Juice from tomatoes, lemons, and other citrus fruits are great exfoliants. Exfoliants help to remove dead skin cells and open up pores. Lemon juice applied to the face with a cotton ball and left for ten minutes is especially effective.
- Chilled green tea splashed on the skin works as an astringent and calms irritation.

The fact that you can purchase over-the-counter products and natural remedies without a doctor's prescription does not mean that you should use them without care. Follow any instructions and start off slowly to see how your skin reacts. If your skin becomes irritated, wait and try another remedy.

WHEN TO SEE A DERMATOLOGIST

What if you've tried different over-the-counter acne products and your skin still isn't getting better? Many complexions won't respond to at-home treatments. If your skin hasn't responded to over-the-counter products after two months, it may be time to see a doctor. If you are experiencing any of the following problems, make an appointment with a dermatologist.

- Acne lesions are large, hard, and painful.
- You have severe red or purple inflammation.

- Acne is causing dark patches on the skin.
- Scars are developing as acne lesions heal.
- Acne is affecting your outlook on life.

It may be hard to open up to someone about your acne. Remember that dermatologists see skin problems every day in teens and other patients of all ages. Your skin is probably no worse than the skin of the person who was sitting there before you.

A dermatologist may prescribe either a single medication or a combination of medicines. These medications may be topical or oral (taken by mouth). Prescription acne medications help normalize the shedding of skin cells and kill the bacteria that contribute to acne. They are often stronger and more effective than OTC preparations.

Your dermatologist might also use one of several in-office treatments. These include cortisone injections to diminish inflamed cysts and heal lesions; acne surgery to remove lesions with an extractor; light and laser therapies; and other treatments. No matter how severe your acne is, there are plenty of treatment options to consider with a doctor. One is probably right for you!

10 GREAT QUESTIONS TO ASK A DERMATOLOGIST

1 When will my skin condition clear up?

2 How can I avoid stress so that my skin condition improves?

3 Could oral medication help me? Are there side effects?

4 What other treatments are available for my condition?

5 Are there other things I can do to improve my skin condition, such as changing my diet?

6 Is my skin condition hereditary?

7 How can I decrease flare-ups or breakouts?

8 Are the over-the-counter products I am using contributing to my condition?

9 Should I avoid cosmetics?

10 Should I avoid wearing certain types of fabric?

CHAPTER four

OTHER SKIN CONDITIONS

Chances are, you've already been to a dermatologist if you have serious acne or another condition such as eczema or psoriasis. Although these conditions are unpleasant, they are not uncommon. This chapter will raise your awareness of skin diseases that can be annoying or even life threatening. A little bit of knowledge will go a long way toward keeping your body's largest organ comfortable and healthy.

SKIN CANCER

Skin cancer is one of the most common types of cancer in the United States. Skin cancer occurs because of mutations, or changes, in the DNA in cells. These changes cause cells to reproduce and grow abnormally. In skin cancer, UV light from the sun is the main cause of the genetic mutation. The three main types of skin cancer are basal cell carcinoma, squamous cell carcinoma, and malignant melanoma. Malignant melanoma is the most dangerous.

Skin cancer most commonly occurs on areas of the skin exposed to the sun. For this reason, you should use sunblock when exposed to the sun and avoid artificial tanning devices and machines, which expose the skin to ultraviolet light.

Skin cancer is first detected when a doctor or patient sees lesions on the surface of the skin. Melanoma lesions usually start off as pigmented moles that, over time, begin to change in size,

According to the American Academy of Dermatology, the use of indoor tanning beds is associated with an increased risk of skin cancer. Girls and women make up about 70 percent of regular tanners.

shape, or color; become itchy; or begin to bleed. Basal cell carcinoma often occurs as pearly papules (bumps), often with tiny superficial blood vessels on top. They often appear at the top of the ears. Squamous cell carcinoma appears as a hard, crusty, scaly patch, usually with an ulcer (open sore) in the center and raised edges. These types of cancer are easily treated and cured. However, they can be dangerous if left untreated.

Malignant melanoma is cancer of the melanocytes, which are cells that make melanin, the substance that gives skin its color. Melanoma lesions are normally pigmented in shades of brown or black, appearing to be moles. However in about 10 percent of cases, the melanoma is unpigmented, or flesh-colored. Malignant melanoma can metastasize, or spread, to other parts of the body. The cancer can invade other organs if not treated promptly and can become life threatening.

The most serious of the skin cancers, malignant melanoma often involves a mole that begins to bleed or that changes in color or shape. If it is not caught early, melanoma can be fatal.

DETECTING AND TREATING SKIN CANCER

Early detection is the best weapon in fighting skin cancer. Carefully watching suspicious moles is a good start. If you see a mole or patch that is irregular, is growing larger, is not all the same color, or is changing over time, you should see a dermatologist who can determine if the mole is cancerous.

If the dermatologist suspects that you have skin cancer, he or she may perform a biopsy. A biopsy is the removal of a small amount of tissue, which is examined in a laboratory to look for cancerous cells.

The most common treatment for skin cancer is removal of the cancer, plus a small amount of the surrounding tissue, to reduce the chance of the cancer recurring. In some cases of malignant melanoma, surgery is combined with treatment by radiation or chemotherapy. In radiation treatment, a beam of energy is used to destroy cancer cells. In chemotherapy, one or more very powerful medications are taken orally or intravenously (through a vein). These medications kill fast-growing cells, including cancer cells, wherever they are in the body. Chemotherapy is most commonly used when the cancer is suspected of spreading to other parts of the body.

PSORIASIS

Skin cells are normally shed in about thirty days. New skin cells gradually move from lower to higher layers of skin, replacing old skin cells as they are sloughed off through normal wear. In psoriasis, however, instead of gradually maturing, skin cells quickly move to the surface of the skin over three to six days. They build up on the skin's surface, forming scaly pink or white patches called plaques. Plaques occur most commonly on the hands, feet, elbows, knees, scalp, and lower back.

The cause of psoriasis is unknown, though the condition can be inherited. It is thought to be an autoimmune disease, or a disease in which a person's body inappropriately attacks itself. Medications that block the activity of the immune system often help. Cold weather, stress, skin injuries, infection, and some medications can make psoriasis worse. Although there is no cure for psoriasis, the symptoms can be improved by using

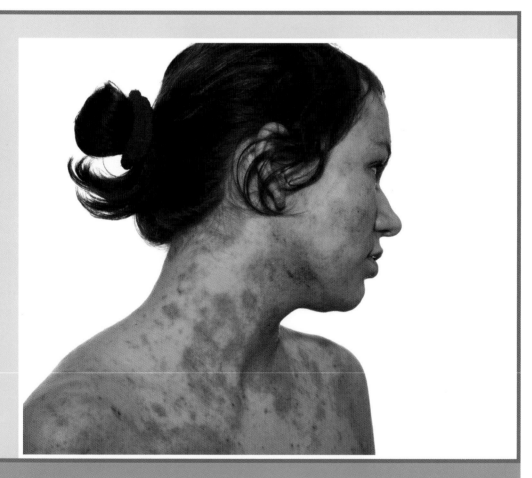

Eczema, also known as atopic dermatitis, is a skin condition that can have severe flare-ups. According to the Mayo Clinic, it is likely caused by a malfunction of the immune system.

topical ointments and creams, phototherapy (light treatment), and oral medication prescribed by your doctor.

ECZEMA

One of the most common skin conditions is eczema, which results in dry, red, itchy skin. It occurs most frequently in people with a family history of allergies. Triggers for eczema include stress, contact with substances to which a person is allergic, irritation from cleaning and skin-care products, and irritation from environmental and climatic conditions. Mild cases can be treated with an over-the-counter cortisone cream. Serious cases of eczema are usually treated with prescription-strength cortisone ointments or shots, phototherapy, antihistamines (a type of medication used to treat allergies), and immunosuppressant drugs to lower immune system activity.

WARTS

Warts are a type of noncancerous skin growth. They occur when the human papillomavirus (HPV) gets into the top layer of skin through a crack or break in the skin. This causes the skin cells to grow abnormally fast, resulting in a raised bump. Most common warts eventually go away by themselves over time because your immune system eventually destroys them. If a wart is embarrassing or annoying, a dermatologist can remove it. One of the most common ways of removing warts is by cryotherapy (freezing).

By following the tips provided in this book, you can decrease your chances of getting skin diseases and deal constructively with any conditions that do occur. Care for and protect your skin, and it will keep working for you for many years to come.

GLOSSARY

acne A skin disease caused by inflammation of the sebaceous glands and hair follicles, often causing the formation of pimples.

alpha-hydroxy acids (AHAs) Natural acids found in fruit, sugarcane, and milk that help to get rid of dead skin cells.

androgen A male sex hormone produced by the body, present in both males and females.

antiseptic Something that helps prevent infectious microorganisms from growing.

astringent A substance used to remove excess oil from the skin and close pores after cleansing.

benzoyl peroxide A compound that kills the bacteria associated with acne.

blackhead A clogged pore (comedo) with a dark center, which results from the oxidation of the material clogging the pore.

comedo A pore clogged with a plug of sebum.

cortisone A medicine that reduces inflammation.

cyst A large, painful lump filled with fluid or pus that forms deep under the skin's surface in the dermis.

dermatologist A doctor who specializes in treating skin diseases, including acne.

dermis The thick inner layer of skin beneath the epidermis.

epidermis The protective outer layer of the skin, covering the dermis.

exfoliant A substance used to remove dead skin cells and open up pores.

extractor A small, metal, circular instrument that a dermatologist centers on a comedo to push down surrounding skin, causing the plug to extrude.

hair follicle A tiny duct in the skin where hair grows.

lesion An infected or diseased patch of skin.

nodule A cyst.

noncomedogenic Referring to oil-free products that should not clog pores and cause acne.

papule A raised red bump where the skin has become inflamed.

pore A tiny opening in the skin through which sweat or sebum reaches the skin's surface.

pustule A raised red bump filled with pus.

salicylic acid A medicine that loosens the plugs in clogged pores and normalizes the shedding of dead skin cells.

sebaceous gland A gland that produces oily matter, called sebum, for lubricating hair and skin.

sebum Oily secretion of the sebaceous glands that acts as a lubricant for the hair and skin.

sulfur A natural antiseptic added to some soaps to help prevent bacteria from growing.

T-zone The area of the face that runs across the forehead and down the nose to the chin.

tea tree oil A natural tree oil that helps kill bacteria.

topical Used or applied on the surface of the skin.

whitehead A closed, clogged pore that forms a tiny bump with a white center.

FOR MORE INFORMATION

American Academy of Dermatology (AAD)
P.O. Box 4014
Schaumburg, IL 60168
(866) 503-SKIN [7546]
Web site: http://www.aad.org
The AAD is committed to advancing the diagnosis and medical, surgical, and cosmetic treatment of the hair, skin, and nails. The organization's Web site provides a range of information on a variety of dermatology topics, including acne.

American Skin Association
346 Park Avenue South, 4th Floor
New York, NY 10010
(800) 499-SKIN [7546]
Web site: http://www.americanskin.org
The mission of the American Skin Association is to advance research, champion skin health—particularly among children—and raise public awareness about skin disease.

Canadian Dermatology Association (CDA)
1385 Bank Street, Suite 425
Ottawa, ON K1H 8N4
Canada
(613) 738-1748
Web site: http://www.dermatology.ca
The CDA exists to advance the science and art of medicine and surgery related to the care of the skin, hair and nails.

Canadian Skin Cancer Foundation (CSCF)
#780 10665 Jasper Avenue
Edmonton, AB T5J 3S9
Canada
(780) 423-2723
Web site: http://www.canadianskincancer.com
The CSCF provides outreach and education for the prevention and
early detection of skin cancer.

National Eczema Association (NEA)
4460 Redwood Highway, Suite 16D
San Rafael, CA 94903-1953
(800) 818-7546
Web site: http://www.nationaleczema.org
The mission of the NEA is to improve the health and quality of life of
individuals with eczema through research, support, and education.

WEB SITES

Due to the changing nature of Internet links, Rosen Publishing has
developed an online list of Web sites related to the subject of this
book. This site is updated regularly. Please use this link to access
the list:

http://www.rosenlinks.com/gh/skin

FOR FURTHER READING

Bergamotto, Lori. *Skin: The Bare Facts*. San Francisco, CA: Zest Books, 2009.

Brezina, Corona. *Frequently Asked Questions About Tanning and Skin Care* (FAQ: Teen Life). New York, NY: Rosen Publishing, 2010.

Donovan, Sandra. *Stay Clear! What You Should Know About Skin Care* (Health Zone). Minneapolis, MN: Lerner Publications, 2009.

Howse, Emily. *Zitface*. New York, NY: Marshall Cavendish, 2011.

Jaoui, Silvaine. *For Girls Only: The Ultimate Guide to Being a Girl* (Sunscreen). New York, NY: Abrams, 2010.

Juettner, Bonnie. *Acne* (Diseases and Disorders). Detroit, MI: Lucent Books, 2010.

Katz, Anne. *Girl in the Know: Your Inside-and-Out Guide to Growing Up*. Toronto, Canada: Kids Can Press, 2010.

Lluch, Isabel, and Emily Lluch. *The Ultimate Girls' Guide to Understanding and Caring for Your Body*. San Diego, CA: WS Publishing Group, 2009.

Saari, Holly. *Is This Really My Body? Embracing Physical Changes* (Strong, Beautiful Girls). Edina, MN: ABDO Publishing, 2010.

Wassner Flynn, Sarah. *Head-to-Toe Guide to You*. New York, NY: Scholastic, 2010.

Wohlenhaus, Kim. *Skin Health Information for Teens* (Teen Health Series). 2nd ed. Detroit, MI: Omnigraphics, 2009.

INDEX

A
acne, 4, 15, 16, 33–34
  hormones and, 21, 24
  preventing, 28
  natural remedies, 32–33
  products for, 30–32
  types, 26–28
  what it is, 22–24
antibacterials, 8–9, 31

B
benzoyl peroxide, 15, 31

C
cancer, 21, 36–39
combination skin, 17
comedones, 26
cysts, 26–28, 30

D
dermatologists, 14, 33–34, 36, 39
  questions to ask, 35
diet, balanced, 4, 13, 18, 21, 35
dry skin, 15, 16, 17, 19–20, 32

E
eczema, 13, 36, 41
exercise, 13, 18

G
green tea, 33

I
ice, 33

J
juices, fruit and vegetable, 33

N
normal skin, 16, 17–19

O
oily skin, 15, 16, 19

P
papules, 26, 28, 38
picking pimples, 30
psoriasis, 13, 36, 39–41
pustules, 26, 28

S
salicylic acid, 15, 31–32
skin
  information source, 10–11
  metabolism, 12
  myths and facts about, 21
  protective barrier, 8–9
  structure, 6–8
  temperature regulator, 9–10
  types, 16–17
skin-care products, choosing, 4, 14–15,
    28–29, 30–32
steaming, 33
sulfur, 33

ABOUT THE AUTHORS

Sabina K. Jaworski is a writer with a strong interest in health and wellness topics.

Robert Chehoski is an author and editor of young adult books.

PHOTO CREDITS

Cover, p. 1 © www.istockphoto.com/Ivan Bliznetsov; p. 5 Jupiterimages/
Goodshoot/Thinkstock; pp. 7, 9, 10, 14, 17, 23, 37 Shutterstock.com; pp. 11,
30 iStockphoto/Thinkstock; p. 16 Comstock/Thinkstock; p. 18 © www.istockphoto.
com/Fotowizje studio@bartektomczyk.pl; p. 20 Hans Neleman/Digital Vision/Getty
Images; p. 25 © www.istockphoto.com/rollover; p. 27 Antoine Barnaud/Photo
Researchers, Inc.; p. 32 © www.istockphoto.com/Amanda Rohde; p. 38 Kallista
Images/Collection Mix: Subjects/Getty Images; p. 40 © www.istockphoto.com/
Božo Kodrič.

Designer: Nicole Russo; Editor: Andrea Sclarow;
Photo Researcher: Peter Tomlinson